FINAL CALL

by
Anson Hughes

iUniverse, Inc.
Bloomington

Final Call

iUniverse books may be ordered through booksellers or by contacting:

iUniverse
1663 Liberty Drive
Bloomington, IN 47403
www.iuniverse.com
1-800-Authors (1-800-288-4677)

ISBN: 978-1-4697-9971-1 (sc)
ISBN: 978-1-4697-9972-8 (e)

Printed in the United States of America

iUniverse rev. date: 4/4/2012

To Anai, Anail, Anson, Makayla, and Jared

The five important reasons that I pattern
my steps after those of a good man

Acknowledgments

Thanks to my granny, Bennie Mae for believing in me before anyone else did.

Thanks to my mother Christine for teaching me as best she could about life, love and religion.

To my daughter Veronica you inspire me, as you will never know. Thanks for being the big sister that leads by example.

Thanks to my siblings Andre, Lee, Jada, Janetta, Christy, Albert, and Machael. It is because of you all that I know what true love is.

Thanks to Carletta, the inspiring spirit that led to these words being in print instead of the briefcases that imprisoned them for years.

Thanks to Aunt Joyce, Rosa, Kenneth, Dwayne, Tyrone, Bronie, Derrick, Henry, Antonio (Tony), Anthony, Minister Osborne, Nichole, and Keisha.

Thanks to all my friends at Railcrew Xpress and BNSF (Burlington Northern Santa Fe) railroad who knew about this project and showed their support.

A person can do many things in life but without family and good friends being there through it all, it seems like it would be harder, sadder and incomplete to me. Special thanks to you all for making the steps I needed to take easier.

In the words of Bennie Mae Hughes, if I have forgotten to thank anyone, "blame it on my head not my heart."

Contents

"God is the God of the living, not the dead, because all people are alive to him."
—Luke 20:38- (New Century Version)

AFFECTIONATE EXPRESSIONS

Mama

Very demanding, understanding
This woman speaks her mind
Beautiful person, sometimes cursing
To me she is one of a kind
Good advisor, smarter wiser
Than any other family member
Loving care, always there
As perfect as snow in December
Smiling face, warm embrace
Listens without being judgmental
Doesn't brag, sometimes nag
Older but still quite gentle
Extravagant lady daddy's baby
Holds her family together
Strong shoulders, sister soldier
Encourages that things will get better
Child bearer, pants wearer
Sometimes she has to play dad
No sweat, never fret
She prays when things get bad
Knows pain, breaks chains
Has escaped hard times and danger
Easy going, patience showing
Quick to forgive, slow to anger
Churchgoer, seed sower
Believes God is able to guide her
God lover, good mother
Mama thank you for being a provider

The Ways of a Good Mother

Thanks be to God for the mothers that we have
They seem to have an inner strength that lasts' and last's and last's
We know they get weak for they are human too
But even at their weakest points they keep on coming through
They tell us that we can when we don't think we can
A good mother raises her son to become a responsible man
A good mother raises her daughter to become a responsible woman
She teaches her how to hold on when trials seem to keep coming
A good mother loves her children even when they treat her absurd
She teaches them how she was taught to believe in Gods holy word
Even when they go astray looking like they're gone
A good mother prays for their souls, standing with open arms
She would pray if they were in jail or in the streets on crack
She would put her total confidence in God to bring them back
She cries many tears but refuses to doubt or faint
Whether speaking in tongues or swinging her belt, she remains a saint
A good mother is like no other she laughs when she should be crying
A good mother is one in a million it comes naturally to her without trying

The ways of a Good Mother was written in celebration of Mother's Day for my mother in particular. I have always known my mother's love for me, but when I was falsely accused of stealing cars back in the day she had my back never once doubting my side of the story, which illustrated clearly to me the true signs of a good mother.

Grandma

A grandma should be sweet and kind
keeping us ahead if we're falling behind
Her love is great and beyond compare
someone who will always be there
If only in spirit, making hard times better
her voice calm soft as a feather
Her understanding heart shining like gold
older, weaker, carrying life's loads
Her eyes telling stories loud and clear
her struggling victories year after year
Daily thanking God though aged and slow
gains her strength from where only God knows
She is always, patient full of concern
willing to teach if we are willing to learn
She is the mold that mothers and aunts want to be
The root, supporting grandpa and the family tree

I Take You

I take you for my girlfriend
though any fool can see you're no girl
My soul mate my love my joy
if possible I'll give you the world
I take you into my care
with strong arms and hands you are safe
Relax, let down your guard
you are protected within my embrace
I take you as you are
you are the one for me
Some may say that's not much
through natural eyes they can't see
I take you off the dating scene
no more broken dates or late arrivals
I pray one day to take your hand
becoming one flesh as thus says the Bible
I take you for better or worse
accepting the other vows too
Before a cloud of witnesses, family and friends
my answer to you is 'I do'

I love her

I love her…I love her not
I am so confused about this woman
I smell her scent as it lingers in the air
When she is not around and in places she hasn't been
I love her…I love her not
I am sure I cannot live without her
I would protect her with my own life
Or would I, not
I love her…I love her not
She angers me as no one else can
She calms me the same
She is right for me, I think
I love her…I love her not
She speaks to me softly mostly
But sometimes she screams what she feels
I am sure she hates me at times
I love her…I love her not
Maybe a petal on a flower can tell me best
I can't seem to make up my mind
I wonder how she feels about me truthfully
I will put up with everything she does
Right, wrong, or in between
Until she leaves me broken hearted
Or I understand clearly if I love her or love her not

The Fountain of Youth

I approached the most amazing fountain
the sign read Fountain of Youth
It is said that water from the fountain
will make you younger to tell the truth
I cupped my hands in the water
wanting terribly to gulp it down
I watched shockingly as it splashed and
instant rainbows brightened the ground
Before I could sample the water
my wife took my hand
Kissed me softly then confirmed
she had a master plan
She rushed me from the fountain
to home where her plan unfolded
She firmly massaged my shoulders
deep-rooted stresses unloaded
She knew just what I needed
I melted under her touch
like a school boy in a candy store
I couldn't seem to get enough
I begged her sweet forgiveness
then flattered her with truth
I told her she was clearly
my personal fountain of youth

Question Is, Would You? (Spoken Word)

How many are willing to give up their fortune, fame, superstar name
and change their aim from money, honey, and material gain
To teaching love, life lessons, forgiveness, and truth, question is, would
you?
Teach that love is essential, beneficial, unconditional
and give up all of your traditional artificial loves
Like idols, lustful desires, hate that burns in your heart like fire
Consuming you inwardly stressing you mentally, taking its toll slowly but
surely, killing you eventually
Would you risk losing the popularity contest because you're teaching the
ills of guns, drugs and promiscuous unprotected sex?
The opposite of what the popular is teaching, speaking, bringing to the
masses of lower and middle-classes but the youth are listening to
these asses, spitting corruption, destruction, disaster, faster than a
bullet that'll land them in a casket
I'm only sharing my thoughts and asking questions don't be afraid, these
are some of life's lessons
I've had to crash n burn, to learn to live and give; Lord knows I'm
learning still...
Crashing and burning, gotta start from scratch when I thought I had this
one lesson down pat
However when fired at I fired back-to-back to back-to-back to back
Now I'm the aggressor way off track from where God was leading me
to, gotta get back on track and learn better to handle that...some
see where I'm coming from though all have probably been where
I'm at
Back to building and rebuilding,
asking forgiveness and healing,
just keeping it real with God's children
hoping these words will reach millions, billions, trillions
Zillions of youth looking for truth wanting their pangs to be soothed like
Orajel on an infant's tooth
Straight to the root of the problem, the pains are spiritual only truth can
solve them, resolve them and stop them completely not just pause
them, it was lies and deceit that caused them
Now, if I was living high on the hog in the limelight would I be preaching
this, teaching this, believing this, feeding this to you while being a
hypocritical heathenness, they say the love of money is that evil
and devious
So how many are willing to give up their fortune, fame, superstar name
and change their aim from money, honey and material gain

To teaching love, life lessons, forgiveness, and truth, question is, would
   you?
Teach that love is essential, beneficial, unconditional, and give up all
   your traditional, artificial loves, like idols

So Poetic

Poetry rolls off her tongue like waves off the sea
So crisp so powerful so perfect
Every line gives me chills as they crash down over me
So I listen so attentive so worth it
Passionate raging fire burns inside her like verses from scripture
So touching so pure so present
Smooth metaphors and similes rhyme without rhyming what a poetic sista
So talented so blessed so tested
Effortlessly she enters my mentality and soon I see her vision
So clear so bright so flamboyant
Her love, hate, pain, triumphs and trials become an expedition
So she leads so I follow so rewarding
Her quick wit is like Nascar I pray to keep up
So enveloped so engulfed so intrigued
Quiet as a mute I sit eyes wide shut
So moved so excited so pleased
Through a nonchalant tone, she spits words in to life
So intense so creative so bold
As number one fan, I deliver praise like a man to his wife
So appreciative so real so gold
She is better than my best, moves me to be greater
So I stand so infatuated so indebted
Her verses are not merely phrases but energy flowing from paper
So incredible so unbelievable so poetic

So Poetic is a personal, self-explanatory poem for one of the greatest poets I have ever heard, Ms. Carletta Matlock.

Buffy

She has a life is no one's wife
any man would be lucky
Beautiful and smart still a child at heart
bathes with her toy rubber ducky
Men admire her looks she would be a great hook
but isn't looking to be hooked at twenty
She dates off and on nothing serious or too strong
the male figures in her life are not many
She realizes she's a queen has high self-esteem
so she never gets caught up on her looks
Education is her well that will help her to excel
therefore she stays caught up on her books
No babies being born or condoms being worn
abstinence gives her a better chance to make it
No Amos or Andy no flowers or candy
will make her risk her future and get naked
She makes bad decisions but continues to keep her vision
on the prize God has promised her in time
She is still young as beautiful as a song
that the robins sing about, soft and kind
She is more than a girl wanting diamonds gold and pearls
for her eyes are like jewels by themselves
Her hair is always fresh she knows how to dress
so stunning you would swear she has wealth
Yet, she isn't rich nor poor in a ditch
she has seen some hard times like us all
She lives in the city not a neighborhood so pretty
where dead dreams and human life often fall
Some call her a lucky person I call her determined
to overcome every obstacle in this world
So to her I lift my fist and pray more women will be like this
to Buffy I'd like to say, "You go girl!"

Sadly, Learning

Already at fourteen, her heart has been broken
A million tears flow, speaking words unspoken
Her mood distinctly dark like the nighttime ocean
Her smile and good grades suffer through her coping
She wondered why heartbreak felt painful and sickly
She wondered how love could go wrong so quickly
Wasn't love all good all the time she pondered briskly
Why date me and hug me, then hate me and dis me
Does everyone perform on this crazy lovesick stage?
Fall in and out of love at such a tender young age?
"Will I ever love as deep?" she asked herself in the mirror
Her heart answered, "Yes, much deeper stronger and purer."

Sadly, Learning is a poem I wrote with my twin daughters in mind. They have both experienced their first heartbreak and I just want them to know that love is a game of chance. Sometimes you win sometimes you lose, but don't stop playing. Just be careful who you play it with.

INTRIGUING LIFE VERSES

Cause I'm a Black Man

Cause I'm a black man I stand up for my rights
Cause I'm a black man don't mean I hate the whites
Cause I'm a black man I have a beautiful color
Cause I'm a black man I love my sisters and brothers
Cause I'm a black man I don't have too many friends
Cause I'm a black man I have ashy skin
Cause I'm a black man don't mean I carry a gun
Cause I'm a black man don't mean I'm on the run
Cause I'm a black man don't mean I can't be kind
Cause I'm a black man I value God and time
Cause I'm a black man don't mean I steal or rob
Cause I'm a black man don't deny me a job
Cause I'm a black man don't mean I cannot read
Cause I'm black man don't mean I won't succeed
Cause I'm a black man don't mean I cannot spell
Cause I'm a black man I say 'naw and yea'
Cause I'm a black man don't mean I cannot add
Cause I'm a black man some people see me as bad
Cause I'm a black man I have an active mind
Cause I'm a black man I hate the unemployment line
Cause I'm a black man I have to watch my back
Cause I'm a black man my history is black
Cause I'm a black man my woman loves me
Her strong, proud, honest, God fearing black man

Lost

My mind is racin' a million miles per minute
I'm seein' visions of red my head is spinnin'
I'm tied up at the moment and my hands are bound
At one time, I could see now I'm blind, down
I was free to roam to and fro as I pleased
Now I'm in deep water like a ship at sea
I was born a warrior in a tropical land
Now like a sheep against a wolf I'm a helpless man
Still a brave intellect but something ain't clear
Cause I'm afraid of the faces and voices I hear
Partly dazed as if I was dreamin'
There are women children and brave men screamin'
Where did I go wrong I was mighty as thundah
Now am I in hell is all I can wondah
The smell on my body is vulgar and foul
I'm throwin' up constantly and movin' my bowels
'Stand up straight nigga', now I'm really confused
'Cause that's the first time I've heard that word 'nigga' used
I started praying for death, lookin' forward to my grave
Far from home brought to America to be a slave

The poem Lost was, converted into a theatrical skit for a Black History Celebration at End Times Christian Assembly in St. Louis, Missouri on February 27, 2011. I thank the pastor and his entire church family for giving my work a literal stage to be acknowledged. Special thanks to Mattie Vasser and Mattie Dent.

Enough Is Enough

Why my brother, do you stare at my woman when she is clearly holding
my hand?

Why my brother, do you insist to persist when she tells you she has a
man?

Why my brother, do you call her names that pull her radiant smile
down?

Why my brother, do you act like a clown whose mind is not strong, nor
sound?

When she wears tight shorts and pants, you hope to get what you see

When she wears loose skirts and dresses, you still let your imagination
run free

If men treated your mother, daughter or woman like you've treated the
ones you've met

You would be outraged so I ask you, 'Why the disrespect'?

Come Out of Hiding

Why black woman, do you wear a weave or extensions in your hair?
Why do you wear the colored contacts when your eyes are like jewels so
    rare?
Has America made you ashamed of being black, natural and pure?
Is there something inside that makes you feel unsure?
I remember a time when dark skin was thought to be ugly or strange.
That kind of thinking is outdated your beauty remains.
You don't need make-up to aid your beauty you're beautiful as you are.
The facade you choose to enrich your outer looks glares as fake even
    from afar.
If you must change on the inside; let self-love guide you as a woman.
As your glow unfolds, it is like a rainbow and what seemed gloomy is
    now more becoming.
Your beauty comes out of Africa back to the roots of the story.
Be the queen or princess God created so that others may observe God's
    glory.

Maybe This'll Learn Ya

Whuh was you thankin' brangin' a chile in dis wirl
ain't me an' yo pa done tole ya bout lane up wit dese guhs?
We tole ya bout patecshin when we tole ya bout boids-n-bees
an' nigh ya gots a beby dats bone wit some d'zees
we woned ya cause we knowed dese guhs was havin' sess
dey sleep wit choo, sleep wit dat, an 'lookin' fo da nex
erythane dat look good ain't good fo ya son
now ya lookin' dumb cause ya p'nis wonit fun
ya say it huts ya bad ta go an' takes a pee
well it huts me ta see dat dis chile look lack me
ya gots dis chile in a d'zees in ya gal is runnin' wit hoods
I mus amit dat wile guh done rally got choo good

Changing Times

I used to sleep on the porch or camp out in the yard
That's when blacks were all for one, but times were just as hard
Nowadays, I'm not as brave and I barely sleep at all
I pray to God the gunshot fired won't come in through my wall

Miss Matched

The blue-eyed woman approached the car, in which sat the brown-eyed
man
He turned the key as she got in, they rode hand-in-hand
Her long auburn hair danced in the wind while his short grey hair,
remained still
The European woman and African man were racially profiled and killed

Curiosity

She spread her legs for enjoyment to see if all the hype was true
She was never the curious type but soon she would try something new
She heard that sex had it all...an excitement with a sweet kind of pain
She was told that it could not be explained yet, you would want it again
    and again
Being a virgin was a virtuous reward but sex peaked its own curiosity
Could it really be as good as she'd heard?
Yes...no...possibly
She'd been asked to have sex on occasion but never had a steady
    boyfriend
No longer was that the case, for she was infatuated and would finally
    give in
She wanted it more than she expected to and bought condoms as well as
    set the date
When finally alone with her boyfriend she trembled weary from the wait
What she experienced was a dull and achy penetration
Alas, in the heat of the moment
she found no excitement, sparks or lightening...
in fact curiosity had led to disappointment

After hearing lots of young girls and older women say they wished they had waited to lose their virginity, a curiosity was created in my mind. To my amazement, many females have laughed dismissively after reading this poem while admitting they agree with it completely.

Satisfying Secrets

Satisfying secrets are hidden under eyelids that sleep at night when only
you and God know what you've done and why.
Peacefully you rest.
No regrets
no apologies
no stress.
In fact, your satisfying secrets are stress relieving.
Unconsciously you beam while dreaming of the sweet taboo you enjoy
privately.
The unmentionable shouldn't feel so good.
Friends and neighbors think they know you well because your acting
skills are impeccable.
Nobody would suspect you of doing the things that you do.
That's funny because they always tell you to do you and you do.
Like a wild fire you burn out of control until quenched by whatever vice
has your soul keeping satisfying secrets.

My Perpetual Testament (Spoken Word)

I know of people you have killed, made ill
You got'em takin' pills
day after day but they'll never get well
Never is a strong word, the wrong word
Many will not get well, few will
I did get a lot better
But I haven't been the same since the fall of nineteen ninety nine
when you came sickenin' me like swine
Scarin' me and mine, had me on my death bed dyin'
Cryin' out to the divine who kept me alive
When I was losin' my life and mind
Watchin' my health go from great to poor
my weight go from one fifty, one thirty, one ten, one zero four
ninety three, ninety two, ninety one
Lord can I possibly afford to lose any more...
Wait!
Fadin' away in the shade of decay in the grey of the day
Had I lost my way my truth my life, had I lost Christ
who said he'd be there till the end of my life?
Was this the end of my life?
Had I finally made it to the front of the line
God callin' my number, was my time up?
Had the disease Scleroderma, you know the sister disease to Lupus
finally do to me what the streets couldn't do all those years I was in it
when I was pimpin' the dope game like women?
This disease made me the victim, bed-ridden skin growin' tighter lighter
    losin' pigment
facial features changin' quickly, all my joints arthritis stricken
Was I payin' for my sinnin' when disobedient and would not listen?
Now a guinea pig to physicians who all decreed, "You will die soon." but
    I didn't
Still, the pain drained my soul
had my mind cloudy
smoked marijuana, the antidote
'cause prescription drugs were just a joke
At least now I had an appetite, could eat a little and gained the will to
    fight
Heart murmur, stomach ulcer, impotence, hair thinnin',
skin so tight
it started to tear
my elbows and knuckles, hands and arms were bustin' open
bleedin' pussin', disgustin'

I apologize for bein' so raw and vivid but thank God you only have to
    listen, I live it!
I fought suicidal demons at night that said, "Kill yourself, 'cause I know
    you would rather die than to live this kind of life."
I shed great tears, prayed for a cure, had ulcers on and around my ears
Too ashamed to look in the face of my peers, I drew back and hid for
    years
Scleroderma I fight you face to face, still have the scars of that fight
    today
I am battered but better, not bitter but blessed,
refined in the spirit
though I look burned in my flesh
I pray for all those who daily press, especially those who won't survive
    and will see death
'Cause scleroderma is life changin', rearrangin', has no apologies or
    explainin'
I know this experience has taught me patience, no longer do I live my
    days in vain
In stride I ride, glide, and fly so high on wings of angels 'til the day I die
Yes, I fight with all my might 'til the day I die
Even if I cannot make a complete fist or get back the strength I had at
    twenty-six
or the good looks I felt I was born with; I fight so Scleroderma's next vic
knows to fight and not quit

The events in My Perpetual Testament are not fictional. I am actually
going through the agony of this deadly disease. Scleroderma is a
chronic connective tissue disease that involves changes in the skin,
blood vessels, muscles, joints and internal organs. In Scleroderma,
case studies show that 80% of the people affected are women and
the other 20% are men. There is a Scleroderma Foundation but still
no known cure, except for Christ.

INSPIRATIONAL VERSES

Acknowledging God's Work

When the sun comes up, when the sun goes down
I see God's glory in it all
When the moon comes out, when the earth spins around
I see God's glory standing tall
When the green grass grows, when the soft breeze blows
I feel God's love all around
When the snowflakes fly, when the raindrops fall
I feel God's love coming down
When the river runs smooth, when hummingbirds sing
I hear God's voice sending peace
When the clouds form bringing darkness and storms
I hear God's voice make them cease
When the rosebuds bloom, when men walk on the moon
I know God's mercy is revealed
When the bees have honey, when the beggar has money
I know God's mercy is real
When seeds are planted and produce is grown
I see God's patience in the earth
When God's children consciously transgress
I see God's patience at work
When leaves change colors, when mountains stand large
I notice the beauty of God
When the caterpillar turns into a butterfly
I notice God's beautiful job
When nightfalls and all are asleep
God watches over every man
When we are born God knows, when we die God knows
Because God has it all in his hands

I Know of One

Who can make a crooked path straight and give life to dead dry bones?
Who knows where the rainbow begins and ends and calls heaven home?
I know of one
Who can mend a broken heart by sowing true love in its spirit?
Who can quiet the blustering weather so his followers don't fear it?
I know of one
Who can open doors no man can close, close doors no man can open?
Who honors faith and truth then reveals things you were hoping?
I know of one
Who understands every worldly problem from poverty, death or pain?
Who can say they have never sinned and loved everyone the same?
I know of one
Who has knowledge of all things past present and to come?
Who can lift any kind of burden without lifting a finger or thumb?
I know of one
Who lived, died and rose for the world to save the old and young?
I wish I knew of more but thank God, I know of one

The Drink of Life

Who would like a drink? Who would like a drink?
The drink that I am speaking of does not come from a sink
Who would like a sample? Who would like a swallow?
This drink is truly purified but not sold in a bottle
Who would like a taste? One taste could ease your woes
This drink is sweeter than soda and much better than H2O
No artificial colors or flavors have been used
No alcoholic ingredients to leave the mind confused
I have seen it leave side effects of happiness, peace and love
I have seen it work miracles but it is not a miracle drug
It helps the lame to walk and helps the blind to see
It helps the deaf to hear and on top of that it's free
So who will be the first, the first to have a sip?
It will help to mend your heart when it has been ripped
It keeps your soul from fainting and helps your mind stay sound
This drink is better than any gold that man has ever found
Satan fears this drink because he knows it works for real
So don't you feel discouraged no matter how you feel
"Let him that thirst come" are the words of Jesus Christ
This drink is guaranteed to give everlasting life

Biggest Catch Ever

Love took hold like a fish to a hook on a pole
It would not let go of my heart, soul
Some said it was a myth, love did not exist
Still faith insisted that I fish
My catch was unbelievable 'til I showed it to people
They believe now because they see you
I pray that all you catch won't throw you back or reject you
You are one that is uniquely special
I enjoy you as you are, you are tastiest served raw
No fire, no pepper, no salt
In murky water, you found the bait consuming me with lust and hate
You took it away taking its place
Every fisherman, knows there's more fish in the sea…not for me
I have caught the legendary love fish in sweet Jesus

All Things Are Mine

If I ask I shall receive, if I seek, I shall find
If I knock it shall be opened because all things are mine
If I believe in my heart without a shadow of a doubt
that all things are mine then it shall come about
All things are mine because all things belong to Christ
Christ belongs to God who holds the keys to death and life
We are heirs to all things present and to come
The victory is ours and our battle is already won
If I ask I shall receive, if I seek, I shall find
If I knock it shall be opened because all things are mine

Stand

In the heat of the battle God's army became discouraged
spirits were low causing doubt they were sure they were going to perish
They cried out to God, who calmly replied, "Stand still."
Confused they scratched their heads, aware that the enemy was on the
    kill
he had already captured some soldiers and taken them over to his side
With his crafty words and cunning ways, he enticed many to backslide
He promised them worldly possessions: cars, homes and gold
What is a man profited if he shall gain the whole world and lose his
    soul?
The fiery darts of the enemy pursued, destroyed and burned
Although protected Gods army cried out, "Lord, are you not concerned?"
When you've done your all and given your best, trust the Lord and stand
    still
God let everyone of them know, "Yes, this is my will."
Some stood with patient faith, while others went straying away,
since they could not see God fighting their battle they refused to stand
    and stay
Their narrow way became wide, because of disobedience they got lost
The enemy closed in immediately cutting their pathway off
"Onward!" came a shout from heaven to those of them that stood
Afterwards came blessings proving their wait was good
In God trust and obey, you have always been his choice
His sheep He calls by name and the same know His voice
He shows love to all and forgives like no other can
Backsliders and sinners take His hand He is here to help you…
Stand!

A Time to Hold On

There comes a time in this old world when no one knows your pain
A time when your tears are many, when your laughter and joy have been
    drained
Your nights seem longer than your days and all is not well in your spirit
A time when your appetite abandons you, your heart so heavy, you can't
    lift it
Your war cry becomes a low sigh, a moan deep down in your soul
A time when sad songs are sufficient, making more sense now than ever
    known
Encouraging words and cards fall short before accomplishing their task
A time when depression is overbearing 'til you forget this too shall pass
Remember, this is not the end and you're not the first one to face such a
    trial
A time when you must hold your head and press that extra-long mile
Understand it is not going to be easy or fair while travelling this road
Also, know that all of your days will not be bitter and cold
To everything, there is a season and time to every purpose under heaven
Sure, there will be bad times as sure as the days of the week are seven
A time to die; a time to plant; a time to kill; a time to break down
A time to weep, a time to mourn bad times will often be around
A time to cast away stones; a time to refrain from embracing; a time to
    lose and cast away
A time to rend, a time to keep silent, sometimes to keep silent we need to
    pray
A time of hate, a time of war, these times have a flipside indeed
A time to be born; a time to pluck up that plant which started as a seed
A time to heal; a time to build up; a time to laugh and dance
A time to gather stones; a time to embrace; what a time we'll have if we
    stand
A time to get; a time to keep; a time to sow; a time to speak
A time of love, a time of peace, let the weak be strong as well as meek
Do not feel like a failure because your shine is not your brother's shine
For God has made everything beautiful in his time
Take his hand and walk, tribulations will soon be gone
Know there are blessings in your future so now is the time to hold on

Time Well Spent

I prayed as I looked at the sky and everything around me was peaceful
God was watching me from his throne because to God the sky is see
    through
He sees everything there are no clouds or rain that can blur his vision
He has given us many resources and watched us make bad decisions
He said, "Pray." and we pray when our lives slow down and allow us
When sick, hungry or hurt we will pray...oh we will pray when there's
    problems
But when things are fine when our needs have been met through and
    through
we find time for everybody but God and do everything we want to do
Who would like a friend who called when he was desperate and down
But when things were better he didn't know you, refused to come around
God knows this scene all too well I prayed when my spirit was on high
"Lord what can I do for you?" I asked as I looked at the sky

HELP WANTED

The harvest truly is plenteous the harvest truly is great
God is calling for evangelists to help the sinners go straight
Why must the laborers be few when there are dying boys and girls?
Every Sunday the church is packed but who is witness to the world?

HELP WANTED

Where are the evangelists the true witnesses for Christ?
Have we learned so much that we have forgotten it is a part of our life?
We are to witness everywhere unto the utmost parts of the earth
God needs willing workers in the streets as well as the church

HELP WANTED

If you love me feed my lambs if you love me feed my sheep
The enemy is working double time no time for the saints to sleep
This message is first to me, then to you Gods anointed
Saints, God is showing us a sign and the words read *HELP WANTED*

Ready or Not

Last night I had a dream that Jesus came to town
Accompanied by angels as he rode on the clouds
Holding in his hands the Great Book of Life
I started to prepare to leave with him tonight
I spoke to my friends toward whom I held a grudge
Saying I am sorry, friend, it wasn't for me to judge
People were in an uproar running through the streets
I had to reach my mother I'd hurt her something deep
As I ran down her street Jesus called her name
I could not ask her forgiveness and had myself to blame
I cried out for her as she ascended like a dove in flight
"Mama, mama, mama!" Mama kept her eyes on Christ
I watched her join Jesus and my soul said, "Come quick,
we can visit the hospital to comfort the hurt and sick
then help the homeless, visit the prison and church."
So little time with: "What would Jesus do?" printed on my shirt
The Avenues' congested motorists blew their horns in vain
proving I wasn't the only one surprised that Jesus came
Others were ascending more children than women and men
When Jesus' number was counted he left me there in sin
My bags were just too heavy I had missed the first trip to glory
I had heard this day would come but it sounded like a story
Thank God it was just a dream I have time to work
I have time to pray, ask forgiveness, speak to people I've hurt
I have time to accept Christ I will hold him like he's all I've got
Whether saint or sinner remember he's coming back ready or not

Regardless

When no one believes in you
hold your head up and press on
Believe in yourself don't be blue
don't drown yourself in sad songs
Sometimes you will have to stand
in this big cruel world alone
Without one helping hand
when family and friends are gone
Do not throw in the towel
dreams are not accomplished overnight
Your time may not be now
by faith your dreams are made life
It takes determination and desire
to successfully achieve great goals
Keep a burning like fire
in your heart, mind and soul
God has you protected
from the front, back and side
He is with you every second
as a father and a guide
He has chosen you to win
defeat demands you to be heartless
You will be great in the end
If you just press on regardless

When Worst Comes to Worst

When the mountains of despair will not move
When it seems your enemies plans are going smooth
When everything you try keeps falling short
When it feels like Satan has ripped you apart
When his fiery darts have pierced and increased
When you've prayed, stayed faithful but cannot find peace
When it appears your prayers are being ignored or hindered
When it would be easier to wave the flag, surrender
When family, friends and associates all disappear
When the shadow of death has made life unclear
When your radiant spirit is like a dull dark void
When it seems everyone you meet has found joy
Remember Christ said he would not forsake you
Do not let life's challenges confuse or shake you
Continue going through until you eradicate the issue
Going through means there is an exit, Christ will be with you
He is strength to the weak he will lift and console you
He will make a way to escape no opposition can hold you
He will bless your heart when all hope was lost
He will carry you daily, you just carry your cross
He will restore your faith so you can gain and maintain
He will allow you to see your prayers were not in vain
Do not faint when circumstances come like a flood
You're a child of The King yes, his precious love

Change the World With Love

Although the hearts of men are cold with hands quick to shed blood
The saints of Almighty God must show the world godly love
Pray for hurting prisoners that are bound by sin
Those who may betray you, show them godly love doesn't end
Give to those in need because the poor we will have always
Feed them with natural and spiritual food in these last and evil days
God has prepared our way with salvation and joy from above
He has given us more than enough to change the world with love
For God so loved the world that he gave his only son
His son gave his life for all proving the battle was won
It was love that held Christ on the cross not the hammer and nails
The world was changed when Jesus rose, no longer could sin prevail
When his flesh felt forsaken and weak, godly love brought him peace
When this love is in your spirit Satan cannot increase
When people hurt or harm you show love by blessing their home
When they curse you to your face forgive them and keep moving on
Anyone can get angry and in that there is nothing so strange
To love like Jesus is peculiar but the solution for the world to change

Hold on to Your Cross

The sun is going down, don't you think it's time
to forgive your neighbor and let your light shine?
If you forgive him, God will forgive you
but not only forgive him, forget about it too
I know it is hard after all he hurt you
probably threw stones for no reason and cursed you
But you are of a new spirit and have a sound mind
so don't be deceived when you are so close to Zion
Hold on to your cross forgive and forget
lest God remember your trespasses and debts
Your forgiveness to others may change a life
Marvelous things happen in the name of Christ
Recall the love of Jesus and you shall not be lost
Avoid all appearances of evil, hold on to your cross

Going Through

In this world of confusion, we will feel bewildered and lost
We will go through days of darkness always bearing our cross
When the world is doubting God, unbelieving and letting go
We will trust God for his promise holding on to what we know
When the tears fill our eyes and pain fills our heart
Clocks indicating that God won't make it, that our time is running short
When it seems the situation is fragile and about to break
Know God does not come early neither does he come late
As Job said in the days when his treasures were doubled
"Man that is born of a woman is of few days and full of trouble"
Know there is going to be troubles, tribulations, trials and burdens
Many falling off at the wayside are doubters living a life uncertain
At the end of our darkness we have a brilliant light
The Word tells us we are more than conquerors through Jesus Christ

No Pain, No Gain

No pain, no gain is what I was taught
To be successful in life you must suffer
When the going gets tough the tough get going
When it gets worse, they get tougher
Tough people hold their ground
Until tough times fade away
Just because you're down today
Does not mean you are down to stay
Nothing great comes easy in life
We sacrifice to show we have grown
Psychologically, failure prepares us
for let downs that come later on
We groom ourselves as children
When they first begin to walk
They endure the hurt and frustration
the slips, the stumbles and falls
Soon they relax, stand, and walk
not wanting to sit, scoot, or crawl
Pressing past bumps and bruises
Bouncing back until it all pays off
We must realize it is alright to cry
Just don't give up or faint
Crowns of Life will be given
to persistent faithful saints
Jesus set the perfect example
Being scorned, crowned with thorns
Allowing soldiers to spit in his face
He kept quiet while holding on
They beat him until he bled
Ripped his clothes from his person
Although they killed his earthly flesh
He gained eternal life for certain
Before long every knee shall bow
Every tongue shall confess his name
He lived and died by the rule I was taught
No pain, no gain

Predestined

Before we were, formed in our mother's womb
God predestined our life
We were in his will with a history
With no choice for which side we would fight
With loving patience the Lord created
Never surprised by our many sins
We stumbled along foolishly
He rescued us again, and again
He believed in us at our worst
Disobedient, obnoxious and wild
He exclaimed to the heavenly angels
"Surely I have chosen this child.
He may curse, lie and steal now
But my Son has died for this cause."
God spares us in spite of our iniquities
When content behind enemy walls
Our transgressions and failures mounted
But our Father didn't doubt us one bit
Planting seeds of his Word in our hearts
Slowly pulling us from Satan's old pit
No matter how far we strayed
When we partied, drank and smoked
God stayed true to his word
Honoring every promise and oath
He knows our family and friends
Born in and out of wedlock
Our future, present and past
Our indiscretions to him is no shock
He continues to wait while we wander
He wills us to accept or reject him
If you are his he will call you by name
For your life has been predestined

The Storm

I felt the wind come rushing in
dust, rocks and debris swirled by
The sun played hide-n-seek in the clouds
as cats and dogs poured from the sky
Thunderous roars shook the ground
lightning flashed north and south
The streets became like rivers of water
overrunning the sewers great mouth
Mother Nature unleashed her fury
darkness covered sky and ground
She forced her way through windows and doors
breaking the barriers of sound
Rooted trees tumbled like bushes
violently ripped from the Earth
Fear held my brave heart hostage
my life needed resurrection or rebirth
I remembered Jesus asleep in the ship
when his disciples thought they would die
Jesus lifted his arms said, 'Peace be still.'
The storm obeyed without understanding as you and I
My problems, worries, misunderstandings and trials
Had escalated, threatening me with harm
But once I cast my cares on Christ
he delivered me from the fierceness of the storm

Mercy Is For All

I've committed fornication, lusted and lied
Wished death upon others and thought about suicide
Sold drugs and dead dreams to my own kind
Laughed in the face of the deaf and blind
Stole things I didn't need watched my friends bleed
You cannot get fresh fruit out of a bad seed
As dirty as the earth where seeds are planted
I uprooted and started taking people for granted
As long as I had mine, it really didn't matter
Starving men could not have crumbs off my gold platter
My heart was like stone in arctic cold
Mama raised me well but Satan played his role
Like a fly in a web, sin captured my heart
Heinous sins I committed tore my mother apart
First, she did not believe it then the truth made her cry
When I think about it, I get a teary eye
Men have beat me jailed me and cursed me
for my evil deeds but God had mercy on me

The X-Factor

Painted in darkness, groomed in iniquity
sown in poverty, chained in filth
suffixed in hatred, drowned in sorrow
smeared in doubt, lost in loneliness
hammered with lies, filled with disdain
wreaking with disappointment, overcome with anger
swollen with arrogance, over-flowing with jealousy
blind with foolishness, drawn with temptation
engaged with lust, pierced with sickness
consumed with failure, faced with adversity
intoxicated with violence, stirred with confusion
poisoned with malice, bursting with tears
haunted by demons, swallowed by fear
visited by suicide, suffocated by weakness
judged by hypocrites, threatened by enemies
betrayed by friends, abandoned by family
sinner by nature.
Found by:
The Way
Freed by:
The Truth
Saved by:
The Life
Christ: the X-Factor.

The Door

Physically, spiritually, emotionally drained
Distress in my heart, soul, brain
Pain explores every element of my being
I cry for help but no one sees me
or hears me..."Hear Me!" I stand alone
Knocking on the door, is nobody home?
I begin to kick the unanswered door
That hasn't been answered now or before
Hoping it will open, Simon says, "Open!"
Christ said, "Knock and it, shall be opened!"
What could it be?
It won't open for me
Am I under God's curse?
Because I only go to church
any given Sunday and not every Sunday
Do I have freewill or does God *run* me?
Has he decided not to open the door?
I believe His word, isn't his love evermore?
Why question his justice he is truth after all?
His Holy decision represents the final call
Hopeful I knock feeling doomed for sure
For my blessing lies behind this godly door
that impedes the peace that I cannot reach
Must I go to church every single week?
Against my will to receive my blessing
Will my door then open without any question?
Will my hurt stop and I prosper with wealth?
Seems I'm being punished for being myself
I know it is God because his power is showing
Only he can close doors so that no man can them open
I will continue to knock until Jesus heeds me
Faith forces me to wait for Jesus to free me
At the door

Steps of a Good Man

Before we men, go stepping off in any and all directions
Let's get orders from the Lord, staying in his divine protection
He will not lead us astray if we obey and stay his course
His word has left examples of good men that went before us
God gave Noah steps when he told him to, "Build The Ark"
Noah was a good man his steps ordered by the Lord
I purport to be like Job whose times of trials grew tougher
His wife told him curse God and die; faithfully Job suffered
Moses had to trust God when Israel doubted and cried
Removed his shoes, got commandments from the holy side
Men of battle like Joshua and David never trusted in the sword
Putting many to flight and death, their steps ordered by the Lord
If you are a good man God will order your steps
You can sleep in the midst of lions like Daniel and know you are kept
Tie your shoes and follow the patterns of Isaac, Jacob and Elisha
Isaiah, Ezekiel, Jeremiah, Peter, Paul and Elijah
Abraham, Lot, Luke, this list goes on and on
Jonah, Amos, Hosea, Samuel, Timothy and John
There is one that lived in the flesh not once committing sin
Gave his life for sinners salvation for women and men
Rose from death on the third day his father being his help
Jesus left footprints for all to follow his steps

'Tis the Season

'Tis the season to be giving
Remember the needy and poor
Although we've given all year long
'Tis the season to give more
'Tis the season to be friendly
The sick and shut-in could use a hug
The stranger could use a soft-spoken word
'Tis the season to demonstrate love
'Tis the season to be caring
Let your prayers be for every man
Encourage the heart of the widow
'Tis the season to lend a hand
'Tis the season to forgive
I would say peace is better than wealth
Forgive and you shall be forgiven
'Tis the season to humble thyself
'Tis the season to be jolly
Thank God for what's going on
The real reason for the season
'Tis the season Christ was born

The Meaning of Christmas

"What is the meaning of Christmas?" A woman asked her young son
"Christmas is about Santa bringing toys so kids can have fun."
"No, no," corrected his father on the edge about to shout
"Christmas is watching football, now that's what Christmas is about!"
"I don't think so," exclaimed granny walking around in her gown
"Christmas is about the parade we're going to later, downtown."
The woman was much displeased so she went to ask her daughter
Who was preoccupied at the time splashing her dolls in the water.
"Christmas is about love and the birth of Jesus Christ."
The woman looked surprised and tears filled her eyes.
She was rejoicing in her spirit because the answer was finally told.
More than that it was told by her baby, the three-year old.

COMPASSIONATE VERSES

Cry

Cry! God told me to tell you to cry.
He told me to tell you that he knows your name,
your hurt, your struggle, your pain.
Let your emotions show, let your emotions flow
let your emotions go become *emotional*
Stop trying to hide, trying to confide
in people that tell you, "Don't cry."
Cry, sob, whine, boo-hoo
Because it's you going through…whatever you're going through.
A divorce, an illness, a death
Jesus cried while in this flesh.
Trouble cometh to every person that is born
lies, scandal, betrayal, scorn.
When emotions are locked inside your heart like a pin,
then comes anger, hatred or revenge!
Cleanse your mind and soul with a cry
knowing your father is standing by.
He is not going to stand by too long
Watching one of his own weep and moan.
He loves his kids and has all power
We are his and he is ours.
Until you're able to take it and make it,
moan and hold on…get hit and not quit,
smile through trials, lift your arms in the storm…then cry.
Although you want to appear tough all seasons
or want to appear brave for all reasons.
As a wise man once said in his teachings
"As long as we're crying there is a God above that knows we need him."
So cry.

Abrupt Departure

no farewell dinner to bless her departure.
no last good-byes hugs or kisses to signify she was leaving for paradise.
no family members or friends saying,
"Have a safe trip,"
"I love you,"
"I'm going to miss you, hurry back."
no none of that.
no ticket purchased for plane, train, or ship to take her to a serene
    destination.
no signs of cash withdrawals, clothes being packed or conversations
    about travel to inform loved ones of her journey.
no shopping sprees planned, hotels reserved or restaurants mentioned
    that one might think could enhance this once in a lifetime
    experience.
nobody on earth could delay or cancel the sweet escape that eventually
    took *her* by surprise.
only God knew how urgently she needed to rest undisturbed.
she inhaled softly, exhaled peacefully then unknowingly closed her eyes
    abandoning consciousness.
no welcome home dinner was planned for her return.

Abrupt Departure was written for my best friends and all those who
have lost a female loved one in this unpredictable natural life.

For My Aunts

The yellow ball of heat shined in the sky all day as I sweated looking for
  shade
At night it showered, got cool and damp. Sick and congested I laid
Aunties you are blessed because you will never be sick again
The hardest part of life is death you all got past it, relax and grin
Watch us as your spirit soars no more running your journey is over
No more heat or rain your days are simple while mine grow hotter and
  colder
You all are content all day I'm waiting for that day for now I'm hurting
  and regretting
No more worry, stress, pain or tears everything you're missing I'm
  getting
It's fine I'm not mad because it gave me a chance to write you a short
  poem
To my three beautiful aunts Margie, Barbara and Annetta, you are still
  here even if you are gone

God's Gift Is Love

God planted love and Virginia was born
Love nurtured her through the years
Love helped her blossom like a flower
Love was there sun, rain, joy, or tears
Love gave life to her spirit
Love knew her better than us all
Love opened her heart to be humble
Love taught her to obey God's laws
Love moved mom to love others
Love made mom a good wife
Love gave life to mom's children and grand's
Love overwhelmed mom's life
Love shined through in pleasure and pain
Love gave her strength to hold on
Love multiplied when mom cried
Love always takes care of its own
Love caused mom to be, loved
Love told her, "You can now rest."
Love wants us to know sickness did not take mom
But it was God that loved mom to death

A Faithful Woman

Iola Glenn carried herself as a woman belonging to Christ
Because God made her a head, she refused to be a tail in life
Her words were very real, full of truth knowledge and wisdom
Life's woes or challenges never stopped her from living as a Christian
Saved sanctified and filled up with God's Holy Ghost power
made her strength superior because it came from her Heavenly Father
A mother, teacher, soldier for Christ faithful in deeds and acts
Not just talking the talk, but living it and walking it like that
So kind, loving, and peaceful she has passed all of life's storms
If you knew her, you know God welcomes her home with open arms

A Tribute

The month was August,the date the third, year nineteen twenty four
A man-child was born but only God knew he would fight a spiritual war
He became a leader leading Gods people to and through battle
With integrity, honor and completeness he stayed in God's shadow
Through the hard times he prayed encouraging God's army to stand
He sacrificed, his family going without proving he was a God fearing
    man
He fed God's army from the Bible concerned about what they ate
Markedly superior in character from grace he went on to be great
Like Jesus, he was not liked by all; nevertheless he won the hearts of
    many
"If you wanna be talked about and not have many friends,"he'd say
    "accept your call to the ministry."
Outgoing, outstanding, outspoken, he spared not bringing the Word of
    Truth
Involved in touch inclined with God's people, he endured by being
    grounded from the root
He set examples for preachers of all ages
served as a pattern to be followed
An original individual when it came to his family, eventually he became
    my role model
A husband, father, and shepherd who never turned a weak sheep away
He sweated blood and tears throughout the years knowing God held his
    ultimate pay
By being raised in the days of segregation, he experienced how it was to
    be least
Like Dr. King, he put his trust in God teaching love, brotherhood and
    peace
God saw his servants hard work how he was obedient, faithful and
    strong
Like us he was just visiting until God told him to "Come home"
He had run a good race and fought a good fight in spite of the rain and
    storms
In Jesus he found a resting place when he was just too weak to go on
He said 'he saw the light…dreamed of the light' the light at the end of
    the tunnel
He may be gone, but he's surely not forgotten, the late, great Elder Frank
    McDonald

Sorrow (Spoken Word)

Here…gone,
So long so long
Wish you
Didn't have
To go
I will carry
My sorrow
Today
And tomorrow
I am too
Hurt to say
It won't show
Tears, fears
Here's the deal
We never know
When our
Time is up
Certainly hurting
Almost cursing
The person
That left us
Holding
This cup
It is too bitter
To drink
Straight down
So we
Sip it
For days
Months
And years
Their presence
And essence
Is so real
In our lives
We still hear
Their cries
And cheers
Their laughter
Plasters
The walls
We miss

Their voice
So choice
Explaining
Complaining
Telling
Yelling
Understanding
Demanding
And hoarse
Now they
Lay In
A comma
Like state
Sleepy
Creepy
No emotions
Stone faced
As we wait
Running a race
With the rest
Of the rodents
Take me next
Dear Lord
Take me!
How much
More time
Do I have left?
If heaven
Is my destination
I wouldn't mind
The taste
Of death
I came up
On the
Rough side
Of the mountain
Climbing rocks
Grinding
Sweating
Bleeding
Stressed
Like the one
That now lies
In this box
I saw their

Relentless climb
Slipping
But holding on
I'm not sure
If they made it
To the top
Now they're
Dead and gone
Where is
The justice
The peace
The love
Above
God sits high!
Watching
Giving
Living
Loving
Touching us
By and by
Things we
Can't see
Control
Or comprehend
He touch
Fix
Understand
Open
Close
Break
Or mend
He giveth...
And taketh away
Everything has
Its time
Space
And season
A reason
For being
What its being
A time
For dying
And leaving
God's game
God's rules

He started it
He will end it
Were, just soldiers
In this war
Sweating
Bleeding
Being, led
Like sheep
To the slaughter
Told to
Endure!
My faith
Is fading
Quickly
Fix me
Lord Please
Fix me
My hope
Has *L-E-S-S*
On its back
Stay with me
Come get me
I am broken
Hope*less*
Notice me
Losing
My focus
Holding
Back tears
That stole
My joy
If I cry
I'll cause
A disturbance
Lord
Send me
A plate
Of love
Peace
Mercy
And grace
I've had enough
Of what
The world
Has been

Serving
If I can
Make it
Tell me so
I wish
You didn't
Have to go
I will carry
My sorrow
Today
And tomorrow
I am to hurt
To say
It won't show

Revelations 19

I looked in this nation's eyes and saw no fear of the Lord
Then Jesus came with no warning after He, had been ignored
The heavens opened up like stage curtains blown with force
The one called *Faithful and True* was center stage on a white horse
The once content Almighty was ready to judge at last
Ready or not, here He stood His feet resembling fine brass
He wore a vesture dipped in blood, on His head were many crowns
His name is called '*The Word of God*' how redeeming that sounds
On His vesture and thigh was written *King of Kings* and *Lord of Lords*
His mouth was more deadly than His hands, out of it goes a sharp sword
With it He should smite the nations and rule them with an iron rod
He trod the winepress of the fierceness and wrath of Almighty God
He was followed by the armies of heaven also clothed in fine white linen
Likewise on white horses this war had been planned from the beginning
An angel stood in the sun crying out to the birds in the sky
To come gather themselves to the supper that the Almighty would supply
Now the beast, the kings, and their armies on earth were ready to go to
      war
Against Him which sat on the white horse and His army stronger than
      Thor
This battle did not last very long the beast was the first to be taken
With the false prophet that wrought miracles, waking to a rude
      awakening
They both were cast alive in a lake of fire burning with brimstone
The rest were slain by the sword proceeding out of his mouth like a
      tongue
The birds of the air were filled with flesh like the angel had told them
Of kings, captains, mighty men, of horses and those that rode them
Free men bonded, men small and great fell this day to the sword
Every knee shall bow and every tongue shall confess that Jesus Christ is
      Lord

Final Call

A time was given, a date was given
A place was given too
A woman conceived then delivered
God gave life anew
A soul was born into a world
Of sin, shame and death
Family and friends rejoiced
For this child that took in breathe
In the meantime in between time
The child brought joy to many
He probably hurt his fair share
But which of us can point fingers at any
As the days, months and years
passed by like a gust of wind
Everyone seemed to forget
That the life of this child would end
With life comes death for sure
No reason to be bitter at all
This body is not made to last forever
For we shall all have a final call